A HISTORY OF THE UNITED STATES

BOOK ONE: The Colonies in America

Dr. Marilyn Thypin
Lynne Glasner

Consultant

Dr. James P. Shenton
Dept. of History
Columbia University

ENTRY

Entry Publishing Co., Inc.
New York

Acknowledgments

The photographs included in this text appear courtesy of the following:

Library of Congress—pages 1, 3, 5, 10, 11, 12, 18, 20, 23, 26, 31, 34, 38, 43, 45, 47, 52, 54, 56, 59, 61, 63, 74, 79, 81, 84, 87.

The Bettmann Archive—pages 14, 50.

Schomberg Collection,
New York Public Library—page 77.

Maps by Shelley Dell
Cover design by Marjorie Waxman
Edited by Jane Lebow
Photo research by Shirley L. Green

ISBN 0-941342-00-X (series)
0-941342-01-8 (Book One)

Published by Entry Publishing Co., Inc.
Distributed by Book-Lab
500 74th Street
North Bergen, New Jersey 07047
Printed in the United States of America
9 8 7 6 5 4 3 2 1

CONTENTS

CHAPTER 1

The Explorers

Finding a New World

The 1400s were a long, long time ago. People already lived in this part of the world. These people were the first Americans. They lived together in many different groups. These groups were called tribes.

The first Americans did not speak English. Each tribe had its own language. Each tribe had a chief. The chief helped the people in the tribe to live together. He helped to make the laws for the tribe.

First Americans made boats.

The first Americans grew their own food. They used animals for food and clothes. They made homes from animal skins. Most times, they did not use money. When one tribe needed something, it traded with other tribes. One tribe could give corn to another tribe. Then the other tribe would give them fur and other things.

Another part of the world is called Europe. Europe is across the Atlantic Ocean. The people in Europe are called Europeans. In Europe, there are many different countries. In most countries, the people have their own language. The Europeans did not speak the languages of the first Americans.

In 1492, life in Europe was very different from life today. There were no cars, no telephones, no radios, and no televisions. It took a long time to hear about the news. It took a long time to travel. People had to walk, ride a horse, ride in a carriage, or go by boat.

There were no big cities anywhere in the world. Most Europeans lived on farms. A few people lived in towns. The Europeans used coins for money. Farmers came to town. They sold food from their farms. Some of the people in the towns were merchants. The merchants bought and sold things for other people. Other people in the town were workers. Some of them made things.

Some merchants in Europe sold spices. Some spices make food taste better. Other spices help to keep foods fresh. There were no refrigerators to help to keep foods fresh.

Some spices did not grow in Europe. The merchants knew that these spices grew in Asia. China and India are part of Asia. Asia is far from Europe.

Europeans paid a lot of money for spices from Asia.

Merchants wanted to get these spices and sell them in Europe. So they sent men to Asia. These men had to go by ship and then by horse. The ships did not have motors. They had large sails. It was hard to travel by ship. The men also had to travel far on horses. These trips took a very long time. Many people died on these trips.

In the 1400s, European ships had sails.

Some merchants owned many ships. They wanted to go all the way to Asia by ship. Then the trip would not take so long. Their big ships looked for a new way to Asia. The merchants hoped that their ships would come back with lots of spices, silks, and even gold. Then they could sell these things and get rich.

Merchants were not sure that their ships could sail all the way to Asia. People did not know about all the parts of the world.

Portugal and Spain are countries in Europe. People from Spain are called the Spanish. Spain and Portugal had kings and queens. The kings and queens were rich. They could pay sailors to look for a new way to Asia.

Spain and Portugal are not very far from Africa. In the 1400s, many people lived in Africa. These people are called Africans. Many Africans did not look like Europeans. These Africans were black, and Europeans were white. In the 1400s, ships sailed from Spain and Portugal to Africa. Sailors from Europe brought some Africans back to their countries. These Africans became slaves and workers. Some of them worked on ships.

Ships from Europe tried to get to Asia. At first, they tried to sail around Africa. Most sailors did not know the size of Africa. They sailed south. They stayed near the coast. Some sailors were afraid. So they came back.

Other sailors thought that they could sail west to Asia. They thought that Asia was on the other side of the Atlantic Ocean. They had to sail across the ocean. They had to go far from the land. They did not know the size of the world. They did not know about the New World. They did not think that the Atlantic Ocean was so big.

Christopher Columbus

Christopher Columbus was a sailor from Europe. He had some maps. But he did not have a map of the New World. He wanted to go to Asia, too. He wanted to sail west across the Atlantic Ocean. For many years, he tried to get money and ships for this trip. At last, the king and queen of Spain gave him the ships and money.

In 1492, Columbus sailed with three small ships and many sailors. Most of the sailors were white Europeans. A few were Africans. Two months later, Columbus and his sailors saw land. They landed on an island in the New World. Columbus thought that they were in India. He was wrong. Columbus called the islands the "Indies." There were people on these islands. Columbus called them "Indians." But these people were the first Americans.

Columbus thought that these "Indians" were strange. They did not look like the Europeans. They also did not look like the Africans. They had different kinds of clothes. They did not speak the languages of the Europeans or the Africans.

The "Indians" did not have spices. But they showed sweet potatoes, corn, and other foods to Columbus. Columbus and his men had never seen these things. Columbus took some of these things back to Spain. He even took some "Indians" back with him. He wanted to show them to the king and queen.

Christopher Columbus and his men landed in the New World.

Columbus went back to Spain. He told the king and queen about his trip. He said that he had been near India. He did not know that he had landed in the New World.

The king and queen wanted Columbus to sail west again. They wanted him to go to India. Then people in Spain could get more spices. Columbus made two more trips. On the second trip, Columbus and his men landed on another island. Today, this island is called Puerto Rico. Columbus was still looking for a way to India. He never found it.

Explorers from Spain and Portugal

Other sailors from Spain and Portugal wanted to go to Asia. They also wanted to sail all the way there. Rich merchants and kings and queens gave ships and money to some sailors. The leaders of these sailors were called explorers.

The kings and queens of Spain and Portugal talked about the world. They told the explorers from Spain to sail west. These explorers would look for new lands. Spain would own these lands. They told the explorers from Portugal to sail south and east. These explorers would also look for new lands. Portugal would own these lands.

Vasco da Gama was an explorer from Portugal. He was the first explorer to sail all around Africa. The trip took a long time. But he landed in India. He brought back spices and silk. These things helped to make Portugal rich.

The king and queen of Spain also sent other explorers. One explorer was Amerigo Vespucci. In 1499, Vespucci sailed west. He landed in the New

World. Today, this part of the New World is called South America. Vespucci knew that he was not in India. He returned to Spain. He told the king and queen that he had found a new land. Someone made a map of this land and called it America.

Another explorer from Spain was Ferdinand Magellan. Magellan sailed west. He wanted to sail around America. He thought that he would get to India this way. He did not know the size of America. He sailed around South America. He landed on an island in Asia. Magellan died on this island. Then his ships sailed west. They did not land in India. But they sailed around Africa and went back to Spain. The trip took three years. No other ships had ever sailed around the world.

Cortez was another Spanish explorer. He went to another part of America. Today, this land is called Mexico. Cortez and his men left their ships and traveled on the land. First Americans already lived in this land. Some of them were called Aztecs.

Cortez was looking for gold. The Aztecs had a lot of gold and silver. Cortez and his men stole some of the gold. They had many fights against the Aztecs. Cortez and his men had horses and guns. The Aztecs had never seen horses and guns. So Cortez and his men won these fights. Cortez made some Aztecs work for him. He did not pay them for their work. He made them dig for gold. He sent the gold back to Spain.

Other Spanish explorers also went to Mexico and other parts of America. The first Americans told them that there was gold in the mountains. The explorers wanted to find this gold. So they traveled far into the land.

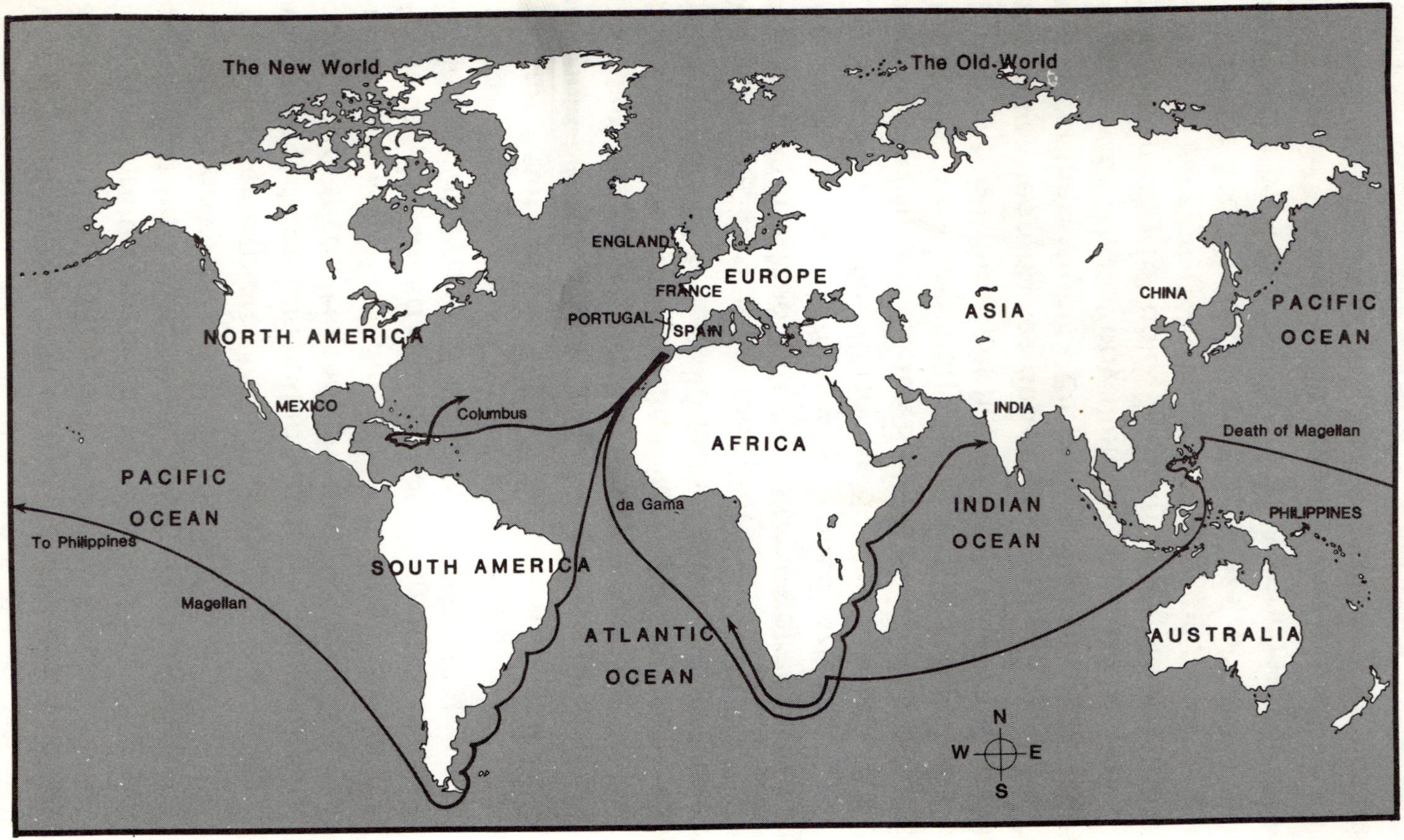
The New World
The Old World
ENGLAND
EUROPE
FRANCE
PORTUGAL
SPAIN
ASIA
CHINA
PACIFIC OCEAN
NORTH AMERICA
MEXICO
Columbus
INDIA
AFRICA
Death of Magellan
PACIFIC OCEAN
da Gama
INDIAN OCEAN
PHILIPPINES
To Philippines
SOUTH AMERICA
Magellan
ATLANTIC OCEAN
AUSTRALIA
N
W
E
S

The World

Some Spanish explorers traveled north of Mexico. Today, this land is part of the United States. Other Spanish explorers went to islands near America. Other Spanish explorers landed on a part of North America. Today, this land is called Florida.

The Spanish explorers had the best ships and sailors in Europe. They brought a lot of gold and silver back to Spain. They helped to make Spain very rich. In the 1500s, Spain became the richest country in Europe. It used the gold and silver to buy many things.

Spanish explorers from Spain went to the southern parts of America. Then the king and queen of Spain said that Spain owned this land. Today, this land is Central America, South America, and part of North America. The explorers from Spain did not think that the first Americans should own this land. They fought against the first Americans. At last, the Spanish explorers and sailors won. For the next 300 years, Spain owned all these lands.

Some Spanish sailors and explorers stayed in America. They were called settlers. The settlers needed many workers to build houses and to work on the farms. But most people from Spain did not want to live in America. So the Spanish settlers wanted the first Americans to work for them. The first Americans did not want to do this work. The Spanish settlers made some first Americans become their slaves. These slaves had to listen to the Spanish settlers. Many first Americans got sick and died. So the Spanish settlers brought Africans to America. These black Africans became slaves.

Some Spanish sailors built little towns in America. These little towns were called colonies.

Spanish colonies were in Mexico, Central America, and South America. Ships from Spain brought horses and other animals to the colonies. These kinds of animals had not lived in America. The settlers used the animals in their work.

The king of Spain thought that he owned the land in these colonies. The settlers had to send gold and silver to the king. The king told the settlers how to live. The settlers could not make their own laws. They had to obey the laws of the king of Spain.

Explorers from France

Another country in Europe is called France. People from France are called the French. French explorers also wanted to find a new way to Asia. Some French explorers came to the northern part of America. They thought that they could go through America to Asia.

Jacques Cartier sailed down the St. Lawrence River.

In 1524, Jacques Cartier sailed down the St. Lawrence River. He made many trips to the northern part of America. Then France said that it owned this land. Today, this land is part of Canada.

Other French explorers also came to the northern part of America. They traveled far into the land. They did not find gold. They found animals. They knew that the skins of these animals made good furs. The Europeans would want these furs. So the French sailors brought them back to Europe.

Some French sailors stayed in America. They made friends with some of the first Americans. They traded with them. They gave some tools to the first Americans. The first Americans gave them furs.

Explorers from England

England is another country in Europe. People from England are called the English. John Cabot was an English explorer. He also wanted to go to Asia. In 1497, he sailed to the northern part of America. Then England said that it owned this land. Today, this land is part of Canada and New England.

John Cabot landed in North America.

In the 1500s, England was not a rich country. It could not pay any more explorers and sailors. But some English sailors wanted to get rich. They knew that ships from Spain traveled to America. They knew that these ships had gold on them. These English sailors stopped the ships from Spain. They took the gold from these ships. They brought some of it back to the queen of England.

Sailors on Spanish ships fought against sailors on English ships.

The king of Spain did not think that England could own land in America. English sailors were taking things from Spanish ships. The king of Spain said that he was angry at the queen of England and the English sailors. So he sent his sailors to fight against England. This fight started a war between England and Spain. Spain had the biggest ships, but the English ships were better. In 1588, Spain lost this war.

After this war, Spain was not very strong anymore. England and France became stronger. English and French explorers made many more trips to America. Then England and France said that they owned some land in America. More settlers from these countries went to live in America.

Europeans and First Americans

In the 1500s, Europeans did not know anything about the first Americans. The first Americans had a different way of life. Their homes and foods were different from homes and foods in Europe. They did not write things down in words. They had their own kinds of religions. They did not go to any church. Europeans thought that the religions of the first Americans were wrong.

In Europe, kings and queens owned their countries. In each country, some people could own some land. Most first Americans did not have kings and queens. Tribes of first Americans lived on some land in America. The first Americans did not think that anyone owned the land. They thought that their gods owned the land.

Europeans thought that the first Americans were stupid. They did not understand the first Americans. They thought that they were better than the first Americans. Europeans decided that they could just use the land in America. They told the first Americans to move. The first Americans knew that there was a lot of land in America. So they moved. Then more Europeans moved to America. They did not think that they had to pay much money to the first Americans for the land.

CHAPTER 2

The English Colonies in America

The Government of England

England has never had a president. England has always had kings and queens. There have been many kings and queens of England. The child of the last king and queen becomes the next king or queen.

The oldest son of the king became the next king.

Long ago, the kings and queens made all the laws. Some rich people in England wanted to help make the laws. The king and queen let them do it. These people started the Parliament. Parliament and the king and queen were the government of England.

This government made all the laws. English people had to obey these laws. Later, the king and queen said that some English people could vote for the members of Parliament.

Parliament and the king and queen made laws about money. All English people had to pay money to the king and queen. This money is called taxes. The taxes paid for the army and navy.

In the 1500s, most English people could not own land. Some English people were very poor. They did not have jobs. Some people went to jail because they stole food. Other people went to jail because they owed money. There were a lot of people in jail. A lot of poor people lived in the streets. After 1600, English people thought that they could own land in America. Then they would not be poor.

In the 1500s, most Europeans had the same religion. They were Catholics. In 1517, people started some new religions. These people were Protestants.

The king of England also started a new religion. In 1534, he said that all English people had to have his religion. All English people had to pay money to his church. But some people did not want to have the king's religion. They still wanted to be Catholics. Other people were Protestants. There were many fights about religion. Sometimes, people were put into jail.

Some of the Protestants were Puritans. Some Puritans left England. They went to another country in Europe. This country is called Holland. In Holland, the Puritans could have their own religion. The law in Holland said that people could go to any church. In Holland, the people did not speak English. The Puritans wanted their children to speak English. They wanted to live in their own land.

Some English merchants traded with Spain. Some merchants in Spain were very rich. They had gold and silver from America. The English merchants wanted to get rich, too. They thought that English people could live in colonies in America. Then the settlers could send gold and silver to England. Then England would be rich, too.

Some merchants put their money together and started new companies. These companies had a lot of money. They decided to send people to America.

The king of England thought that England owned a lot of the land in America. He decided to give a special paper to companies. It was called a charter. The charter said that a company could send English settlers to live on some land in America. But the king still owned the land.

The charter also said that the settlers had the same rights as people in England. Rights are a special kind of law. These laws say what people can do. They also say what the government can not do. Companies could not send people to America without a charter.

In 1606, King James I gave charters to two companies. One company was called the Plymouth Company. This company got a charter for some land in the northern part of America. Today, this land is called New England. In 1606, the Plymouth Company sent some ships to America. The people on these ships tried to start a colony. But they came back to England.

The other company was called the London Company. This company got a charter for some land in the southern part of America. Today, this land is called Virginia and North Carolina.

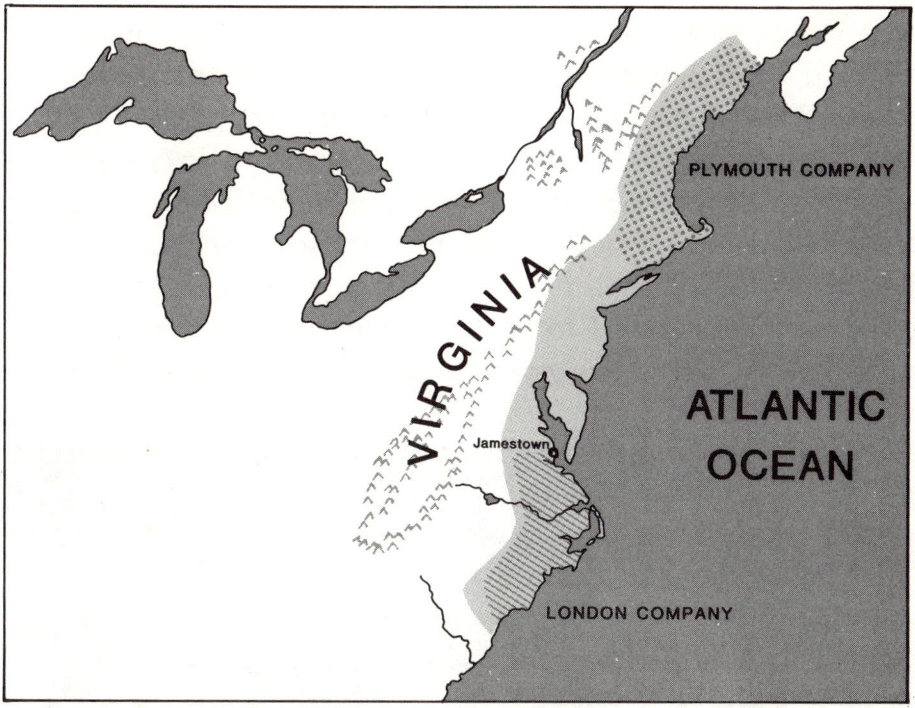

Land of the English Companies

The Virginia Colony

In 1607, a ship from the London Company took settlers to America. Some people died on the ship. Other people landed in the southern part of America. This land was called Virginia. They started a colony. Their colony was called Jamestown.

The settlers in Jamestown had a lot of trouble. The water near Jamestown made many of them very sick. Some settlers died. Some first Americans also lived in Virginia. But they did not have any trouble with the water. They knew how to dig wells. They could get clean water from them. They showed the settlers how to dig wells.

The London Company told the settlers to find gold. Then they had to send it back to the company. The company would pay them for this gold.

The settlers also had to build houses and grow enough food. Some settlers did not want to do this work. They just wanted to find gold and get rich. They did not know that there was no gold in Virginia.

One settler was John Smith. He got angry at the other settlers. He told them that they must work. If they did not work, they would not get food. Then some settlers started to work. Smith made friends with the first Americans. Smith and the settlers traded with them.

John Smith talked to the other settlers.

In 1609, the London Company got a new charter from the king. It said that the company could own some land in America. The company could also make the laws for the settlers. Some settlers owned part of the company. They could own some of the land. Other settlers did not own a part of the company.

These settlers could not own any land. But they could live on it. Many settlers stayed in Jamestown.

In the early 1600s, English people learned to smoke tobacco. They got tobacco from the Spanish colonies. First Americans also grew tobacco in Virginia. They showed the English settlers how to grow it. Good tobacco grew on the land in Virginia. The English settlers grew a lot of tobacco and sold it to the London Company. The London Company made a lot of money from this tobacco. More English people came to live in Jamestown. The colony started to get bigger.

In 1619, the London Company wanted more settlers to grow more tobacco in Virginia. Then the company could make more money. The company sent some women to Jamestown. These women married the men and had children. These families helped the colony to grow.

In 1619, the company also decided to send more settlers to Virginia. These settlers could own some of the land. They did not have to own part of the company. But they had to pay for their trip to America. They also had to grow tobacco and sell it to the company.

The settlers needed more workers. Then they could grow more tobacco. Some poor people in England decided to come to Virginia. The London Company paid for their trip. Then they had to work for the settlers. The settlers did not have to pay these workers. They were called indentured servants. The company would give some land to the indentured servants after four years. Some indentured servants had to wait more than four years. But they thought that they would not be poor in America.

Representatives of Virginia met in the House of Burgesses.

English merchants bought and sold Africans. In 1619, the London Company sent 19 Africans to Virginia. These Africans were also indentured servants. But they had to work for 25 years. Then they could own land. Many black indentured servants died before they could get any land.

The London Company knew that the settlers wanted to make their own laws. In 1619, the company decided that 22 settlers in Virginia could help make the laws for the colony. Then the settlers would have their own government. It was called the House of Burgesses.

Only men could be members of the House of Burgesses. These men had to own land in Virginia. More than a thousand men owned land in

Virginia. So all the land owners had to pick men to be members of the House of Burgesses. They decided to vote. The land owners in one part of Virginia voted for one land owner. This land owner became a member of the House of Burgesses. He spoke for the land owners in his part of Virginia. He was the representative for the land owners in his part of Virginia.

The representatives in the House of Burgesses voted on laws. They made laws about taxes. All the settlers had to pay taxes to the government in Virginia. It paid soldiers with this money. The soldiers kept the colony safe. The settlers also had to pay taxes to the king of England.

More English people came to live in Virginia. The first Americans did not want more English people to live in Virginia. So the first Americans got angry. They fought against the settlers. Many settlers and first Americans got hurt in these fights.

In 1624, King James I decided that he should help to make the laws for Virginia. He thought that he should own Virginia. Virginia should become a royal colony. He sent a governor to Virginia. The governor had to make sure that the House of Burgesses made good laws. The governor could tell the House of Burgesses that their laws were wrong. Then the House of Burgesses could not make these laws.

In 1650, the House of Burgesses made a law about black indentured servants. It said that English settlers in Virginia could own black indentured servants. The settlers would not have to give them land after 25 years. The black indentured servants became slaves. The settlers would also own the children of the slaves.

In the 1600s, there were many different kings and queens of England. Each new king sent a new governor to Virginia. Some governors let the House of Burgesses make the laws for Virginia. Other governors did not let the House of Burgesses make the laws.

CHAPTER 3

The English Colonies in New England

Plymouth Colony

Some Protestants had a lot of trouble in England. They wanted to go to America. They thought that they could have their own religion in America.

Some Protestants were Pilgrims. They wanted to move to Virginia. But they did not have much money. So they talked to some rich men. These men gave ships and other things to the Pilgrims. The Pilgrims said that they would work hard and make their colony rich. They would send things back to the men. After seven years, the Pilgrims would also give some money to these men.

The Pilgrims landed in Plymouth, Massachusetts.

In 1620, the Pilgrims sailed to Virginia. Their ship was called the Mayflower. The ship got lost. It did not land in Virginia. It landed north of Virginia. The Pilgrims called this land Plymouth. Plymouth had hills and good places for ships. The hills could help keep the settlers safe. Today, Plymouth is a city in Massachusetts. Massachusetts is part of New England.

The Pilgrims did not have a charter for Plymouth. The men on the Mayflower decided to write their own charter. They called it the Mayflower Compact. The Mayflower Compact said that the Pilgrims would have the same rights as the people in England. The men would make the laws for the colony. All settlers in Plymouth had to obey these laws.

The Pilgrims built houses, farms, and a church. They did not know how to grow things on the land in Plymouth. They tried to grow food. But they had trouble. They tried to talk to the first Americans. But most first Americans did not speak English.

One first American spoke English. His name was Squanto. An English merchant had taken him to England. He came back to America on an English ship. Squanto told the Pilgrims about the land. He helped them to grow food. Then they had enough food. The Pilgrims and Squanto had a big party. This party was called Thanksgiving.

The Massachusetts Bay Colony

Some other Protestants were Puritans. They had the same religion as the king. They wanted to change some things about their religion. But the king would not let them. So some of these Puritans wanted to go to America. They put their money together and started a company. They called it the Massachusetts

Bay Company. In 1629, they got a charter from the king. The charter said that the company could own some land in the northern part of America. Today, this land is called Massachusetts.

The Massachusetts Bay Company started a colony. It sent many ships to Massachusetts. They landed along the coast of Massachusetts. The settlers started many towns in the colony. Some settlers were owners of the company. Other settlers did not own any part of the company. Women could not own any part of the company.

The settlers needed a government. The company started the General Court. It made the laws for the colony. Only owners of the company could be members of the General Court. The members of the General Court voted for a governor. The governor and the General Court made the laws for the colony. They decided on the taxes for the colony. All the settlers had to pay these taxes.

Many settlers were not owners of the company. So they could not vote. They did not want to pay taxes to the General Court. After two years, they got very angry. The governor decided to change the law about the General Court. In each town, all the Puritan men could vote for members of the General Court. They did not have to be owners of the company. Each town could send two representatives to the General Court. These representatives also did not have to be owners of the company. They would help decide about the laws and taxes in the colony.

The settlers of the Massachusetts Bay Colony had their own religion. They said that the government must listen to the rules of their church. At first, the settlers could not have any other religion. Later, some settlers wanted to pray in a different way. These settlers had a lot of trouble in the colony. They wanted to leave this colony.

Other Colonies in New England

Roger Williams was a settler in the Massachusetts Bay Colony. He thought that the government should let people have their own religions. The government should not tell people that they had to go to one kind of church. Williams thought that the settlers should pay the first Americans for the land in Massachusetts. He was the first colonist to pay them. Williams also thought that all settlers should be able to vote.

The government of the Massachusetts Bay Colony did not think the same way as Williams. It did not want him to talk to other settlers about government and religion. They tried to send him back to England.

Roger Williams went to Rhode Island.

Williams did not want to go back to England. So he lived with the first Americans for a while. Then Williams and some other settlers started a new town. It was called Providence. Today, Providence is a city in Rhode Island.

Another settler in the Massachusetts Bay Colony was Anne Hutchinson. She had her own religion. She wanted to tell people about her religion. The government made her leave the colony. So Anne Hutchinson and her family moved. They started a new town. Other settlers also came to this town. This town was called Portsmouth. Today, Portsmouth is a city in Rhode Island.

Other settlers also started other towns. The Massachusetts Bay Company had a charter for the land in all of New England. The government of the Massachusetts Bay Colony could have tried to make the laws for all of the towns. But it did not send anyone to many of the towns. The people in each town made their own laws.

By 1644, the towns were growing. Williams did not want the Massachusetts Bay Colony to make the laws for Portsmouth and Providence. So Williams went to England. He got a charter for the land around these towns. The charter said that this land could be a colony. It was called Rhode Island. The men in Rhode Island could help make their own laws. Settlers in this colony could go to any kind of church.

The government of the Massachusetts Bay Colony wanted all the settlers to have the same religion. If people did not have this religion, they had trouble. They could not vote or be members of the General Court. So some other settlers left the colony and went to Rhode Island.

Other settlers in the Massachusetts Bay Colony wanted to find better land. Some of them went to live near the Connecticut River. They also got a charter for this land. This land was called Connecticut. Other settlers started another colony. They called it New Haven. In 1662, New Haven became part of the Connecticut colony.

Some settlers left the Massachusetts Bay Colony and went north. This land was called New Hampshire. The government in the Massachusetts Bay Colony made the laws for New Hampshire. But the settlers in New Hampshire wanted to make their own laws. In 1679, the king of England said that New Hampshire could become a royal colony. The settlers could have a General Court. The king sent a governor to help make the laws for New Hampshire.

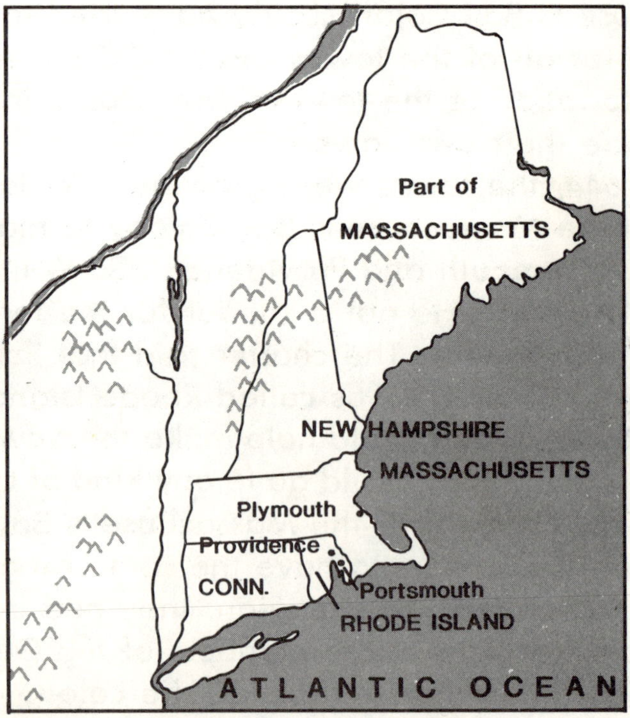

The New England Colonies

Life in the New England Colonies

The New England colonies were in the northern part of America. In the late 1600s, many settlers liked their homes in New England. They were glad that they did not live in England. But the winters were cold. Sometimes, it was hard to grow food in New England. But the settlers had enough food most of the time.

Some settlers were farmers. Other settlers lived in towns. They were workers, fishermen, or merchants. Some settlers built ships or made other things. Other settlers were sailors. The settlers in the New England colonies traded with each other. They did not have to buy many things from England. Sometimes, they also traded with people in England, the Spanish colonies, and Virginia.

The farms in New England were not very big. They did not need a lot of workers. But sometimes, they needed help on their farms. In 1638, some ships brought Africans to New England. The Africans were slaves. Farmers bought them.

In 1641, the government of the Massachusetts Bay Colony said that people could own slaves. Massachusetts was the first colony to have laws about slaves. Slaves had to obey their owners. The settlers did not have to pay them for their work.

Many years later, some slave owners decided that they should not own other people. So they paid their slaves for their work. Some slaves saved their money. Then they gave some money to their owners. Then the owners let their slaves go free. These free Africans had some of the rights of the other settlers.

They could go to the same churches. But they could not become members of the church. So they could not vote for the members of the government.

In New England, each colony had a charter from England. Each colony had its own government. Only men could vote. In most of the colonies, all the voters had to own land and go to the church of the colony. Later, some of the colonies let other men vote. These men had to own land in the colony, but they could go to a different church.

Each colony had a general court. Each general court made the laws for its own colony. Some of these laws said that the settlers had to pay taxes. The government used this money for schools and soldiers.

Some towns had a school. Children went to these schools. The settlers wanted their children to learn to read and do math. Some boys went to school for more years than girls. Then they could read better, do their jobs, and make the laws.

Some towns had another kind of government. Everyone in the town met. They talked about their town and other things. Women and free Africans could talk at these town meetings. But they could not vote. Only some men could vote in the town meetings.

Many settlers came to the New England colonies. The first Americans were afraid that the settlers wanted to take all of their land. They did not want the settlers to tell them how to live. They wanted to live in tribes. Some settlers did not think that the first Americans had the right kind of religion. So they tried to teach the first Americans about their religion. Some first Americans became Protestants. But most first Americans kept their own religions.

The people in Massachusetts had town meetings.

The settlers and the first Americans had many fights. Many people died in these fights. Sometimes, the settlers even took the first Americans and made them slaves.

The settlers in the New England colonies did not think that they were safe. They were afraid of the first Americans and settlers from other European countries. French settlers lived in New France. New France was north of the New England colonies. Today, New France is called Canada.

The people from Holland are called the Dutch. Dutch settlers had also started colonies. These colonies were south and west of the New England colonies. These Dutch colonies were growing. Some Dutch settlers wanted to live on the same land as the English settlers. This land was near the Connecticut River.

In 1643, the settlers in four English colonies sent representatives to a meeting. The representatives were from Massachusetts, New Haven, Connecticut, and Plymouth. These representatives did not like the religion of the people in Rhode Island. So they did not tell the people from Rhode Island to send representatives to this meeting.

At the meeting, the representatives talked about the fights against the first Americans and the settlers from other European countries. The representatives said that their governments would start a special government for the four colonies. This government was called a confederation.

The confederation would start a large army. Men from each colony would be part of this army. The confederation would try to talk to the first Americans. They did not want to fight against them. The government of each colony also had to give money to the confederation. This money would pay for the army.

The confederation talked to the first Americans and the Dutch settlers. Sometimes, the confederation was still angry at them. Then the army of the confederation fought against them. But this army was not very strong. In 1684, the confederation ended. This confederation was the first government for more than one colony in America.

CHAPTER 4

The Middle Colonies

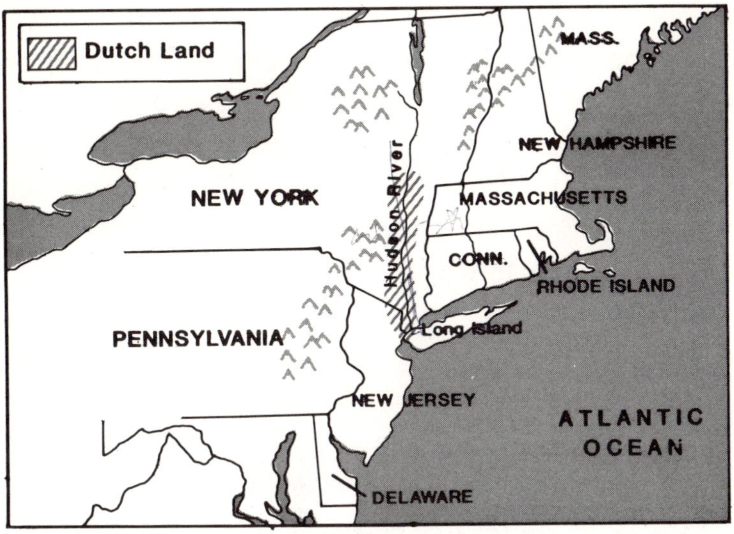

The Middle Colonies

The Colonies in New York and New Jersey

In 1609, Henry Hudson sailed from Holland to America. Then he sailed up a big river. Today, this river is called the Hudson River. The land around the Hudson River is New York and New Jersey. The government of Holland thought that it owned some of this land.

Dutch explorers also went to the land south of the New England colonies. Then the Dutch government thought that it owned the land between the New England colonies and the Virginia colony. But the king of England also thought that he owned the same land on the coast of America.

The Dutch government gave charters for land in America. It gave a charter to the Dutch West India Company. In 1623, the Dutch West India Company sent people to America. The company gave land to some men. Each man had to bring a lot of workers to America. These Dutch men had a lot of trouble. Most Dutch people wanted to own land. They did not want to be workers. But these men found some workers and went to America.

The Dutch West India Company bought some land from the first Americans. One part of this land was an island. The first Americans called this island Manhattan. The Dutch settlers called it New Amsterdam.

Dutch people lived in New Amsterdam.

Some Dutch settlers were farmers. The Dutch land was good for farms. They could grow a lot of food on this land. The farmers needed many workers. So the Dutch West India Company sent Africans to the Dutch colony. These Africans were slaves.

Other Dutch settlers were fur traders. They sailed on many rivers in America. These rivers were the Hudson River, the Connecticut River, and the Delaware

River. The Dutch fur traders traded with the first Americans. They became friends with a tribe. This tribe was the Iroquois.

The Dutch settlers thought that Holland owned the land near the Connecticut River. They built a fort near this river. But the English settlers thought that England owned this land. The English settlers and the Dutch settlers started to fight about this land. The English settlers wanted to get furs from the first Americans. The Dutch settlers did not want English settlers to trade with the first Americans.

In 1664, the confederation of the New England colonies had an army. It started to fight against the Dutch army. The governor of the Dutch colony knew that his soldiers could not win this fight. So he told the Dutch army that they should not fight. He gave all the Dutch land to the English king. The Dutch government had owned a lot of land. It was between the Connecticut River and the Delaware River, and the land on Long Island.

In 1664, Charles II was the king of England. He gave all the Dutch land in America to his brother. His brother was the Duke of York. The Duke of York changed the name of New Amsterdam and the other Dutch land to New York.

The Duke of York owned New York. He sent a governor to New York. The English governor said that the Dutch settlers did not have to leave New York. But they could not have their own government. They had to obey the English government and the English governor of the colony. They had to pay taxes to the English king. The Dutch settlers could go to their own churches. They could still be fur traders in the English colony. Some of them got rich in America.

The Duke of York gave some land to two friends. They called this land New Jersey. In 1664, only a few people lived on this land. They had good farms, but they needed workers. The king of England sent slaves from Africa to New Jersey.

The settlers in New York and New Jersey wanted to help make the laws for their colonies. They did not want to pay a lot of taxes to the English king. They talked to the governors of their colonies. The governors told the king to let the settlers make some of their own laws. But the king said that they could not make their own laws.

In 1685, King James II became the king of England. In 1686, he decided that New York, New Jersey, and the New England colonies would have one government. He sent a governor for all of the colonies. This governor made all the laws for the colonies. King James II closed the general courts in the New England colonies. The settlers could not make their own laws anymore.

In 1688, some people in England and in the English colonies did not want to pay taxes to King James II. They also wanted to help make their own laws. They decided that King James II should not be king of England anymore. They wanted other people in the king's family to be the king and queen. They fought against King James II.

In 1689, William and Mary became the king and queen of England. They said that the people in England and the colonies could have more rights. The people in England could help make the laws. The king and queen gave the charters back to the colonies. They said that the settlers could make some laws in their general courts. But the governors could still say if these laws were wrong.

Pennsylvania and Delaware

In the early 1600s, many English people did not want to have the king's religion. Some of these people had their own religion. They were Quakers. They did not want to pay money to the king's church. The Quakers did not like to fight. They would not be in any army. They also thought that they should be able to speak against the king and his government. When they did, they had a lot of trouble in England. Sometimes, the king sent them to jail.

William Penn was a Quaker. The king of England owed a lot of money to Penn's father. Penn's father died. The king of England still owed the money to the Penn family. So William Penn asked the king for some land in America. Penn wanted to start a colony. He thought that the Quakers could be happy there. They would be able to have their own religion.

In 1681, the king gave Penn a charter for land in America. This land was not on the coast. Penn thought that his colony should be on the coast. In 1682, Penn got another charter for land. Then Penn owned a lot of land in America. His colony was called Pennsylvania. Today, this land is called Pennsylvania.

Penn wanted to make a good colony for the Quakers. He said that people in his colony could go to their own churches. They did not have to be Quakers. Penn also said that people in his colony could help make their own laws. So many Europeans wanted to live in Pennsylvania.

Penn paid the first Americans for the land. He sold land in his colony for very little money. Many people from Europe came to Pennsylvania. They came from many countries in Europe and Africa. They were Quakers, Protestants, Catholics, and Jews. They built their own churches, houses, and farms.

William Penn had a meeting with the first Americans.

Penn's charters said that the settlers in Pennsylvania could help make the laws for their colony. The settlers could have a General Assembly. Some men in the colony could vote for representatives for the General Assembly. At first, all voters had to be members of a church. Later, the General Assembly changed the law. Then all land owners could vote for the members of the General Assembly.

Penn sent a governor to Pennsylvania. The governor could tell the General Assembly that its laws were wrong. The settlers also had to obey the laws of England. They had to pay taxes to the king.

Pennsylvania had good land. The settlers could grow a lot of food on the land. They needed many workers. Some settlers wanted to own slaves. Slaves could help them on their farms. At first, the General Assembly said that the settlers could not have slaves in Pennsylvania. In 1700, the General Assembly said that these settlers could own slaves.

Some people in Pennsylvania did not want their land to be part of Pennsylvania. These people lived in Delaware. In 1701, the government of Pennsylvania said that the people in Delaware could have their own General Assembly.

Life in the Middle Colonies

The middle colonies were New York, New Jersey, Delaware, and Pennsylvania. In these colonies, the settlers lived on farms. Most settlers did not live in towns. The land in the middle colonies was good for farms. The settlers could grow a lot of food on this land. They sold some food to merchants in England and the West Indies.

Some settlers in the middle colonies were friends with the first Americans. Some settlers paid the first Americans for their land. Then the first Americans taught the settlers how to grow food. The settlers and the first Americans traded.

The king of England wanted many people in his colonies. He wanted to have strong colonies in America. He thought that strong colonies would help England. He thought that merchants in England would sell the things from his colonies. Then they would get rich. England would be rich, too.

CHAPTER 5

The Southern Colonies

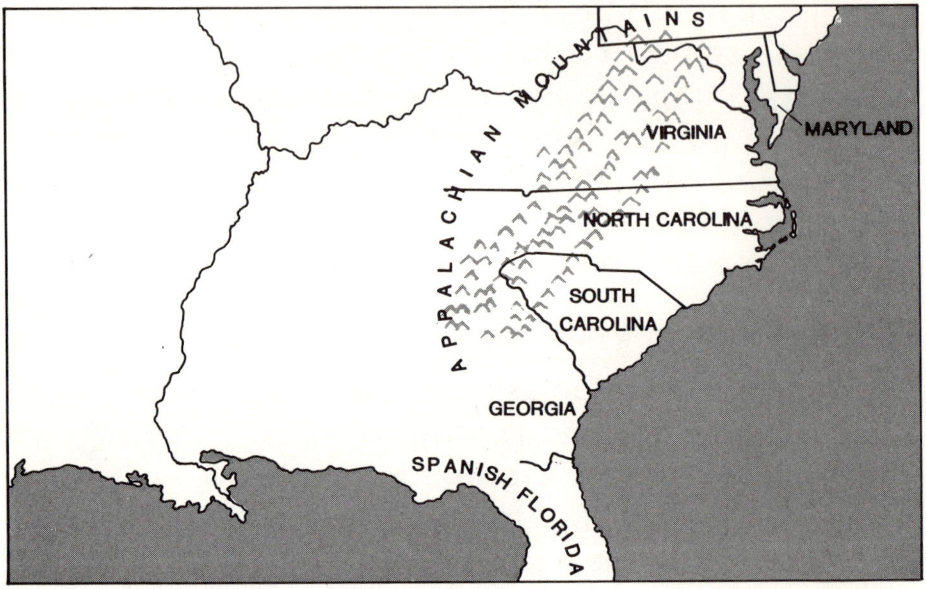

The Southern Colonies

Virginia

In 1609, the king of England gave a charter to a company. The charter said that the company owned some land in the southern part of America. The company sent some people to live on this land. The colony was called Virginia. Jamestown was a town in Virginia.

The king of England thought that he owned more land in the southern part of America. Many years later, the king of England wanted to start more colonies on this land. He gave charters for this land to rich men. Today, this land is called Maryland, North Carolina, South Carolina, and Georgia.

Maryland

In the early 1600s, many people in England did not want to have the king's religion. Some of these people were Catholics. The Catholics wanted to go to their own church. Some English people did not like Catholics. Catholics had a lot of trouble in England. Some of them wanted to go to America.

Lord Baltimore was a Catholic. He asked King Charles I for some land in America. He wanted to start a colony for Catholics. Then Catholics could go to their own church.

In 1632, King Charles I gave a charter to Lord Baltimore. The charter gave him some land north of the Virginia colony. This land was called Maryland. The charter said that the settlers had the same rights as the people in England. The settlers also had to obey the laws of England.

In 1634, Lord Baltimore sent some men to Maryland. These men would be land owners in the colony. Every year, the land owners had to pay money to Lord Baltimore. This money was called rent. Each land owner had to bring five workers with him. These workers were not land owners.

The land owners started farms in Maryland. They paid their workers. The land owners and their workers grew a lot of food on their farms. They sold food to merchants in England.

Lord Baltimore told the land owners that they could start a General Assembly in Maryland. The General Assembly would help make the laws for the colony. Only land owners could vote for the members of the General Assembly. Lord Baltimore also sent a governor to Maryland. The governor could tell the General Assembly that their laws were wrong.

Everyone in Maryland paid taxes to the king of England. The workers gave their taxes to the land owners. Then the land owners sent them to the king. The land owners also sent their own taxes to the king.

Lord Baltimore had wanted to start a colony for Catholics. Many Catholics came to Maryland. But many Protestants also came to Maryland. In England and Maryland, the Catholics and the Protestants had many fights. In 1649, Lord Baltimore asked the General Assembly to make a new law. The General Assembly made the law. It said that Catholics and Protestants could go to their own churches. Then Catholics and Protestants did not have to fight anymore. They could live together in the colony. Settlers would not have trouble because they wanted to go to their own churches.

The Carolinas

King Charles II of England wanted to have more people in his southern colonies. Only a few settlers lived in Virginia and Maryland. In 1663, King Charles II gave a charter to some rich men. It said that these men owned the land south of the colony of Virginia. They called this land the Carolinas. Today, this land is called North Carolina and South Carolina.

In 1669, the rich men sold some of the land in the Carolinas. Other settlers could pay rent for land. The rich men decided that only land owners could make the laws for their colony. Most of the settlers were not land owners. They could not help to make the laws for their colony. The rich men also decided that the settlers could have slaves in the Carolinas.

In 1670, the rich men sent settlers to the southern part of the Carolinas. Some settlers built a town.

The town was called Charleston. Some settlers built ships and traded with people in England. Other settlers built farms in the Carolinas.

Charleston was the first town in the Carolinas.

But by 1670, some settlers from Virginia already lived in the northern part of the Carolinas. They grew tobacco. They sold the tobacco to merchants in England. These settlers from Virginia did not want to pay rent to the land owners in the Carolinas.

In 1677, many settlers in the Carolinas fought against the land owners. These settlers wanted to make the laws for their colony. The land owners did not want to fight against these settlers. But the land owners did not think that all settlers should make the laws for the colony.

In 1729, the land owners sold the colony to the king of England. He decided that the Carolinas should become two royal colonies. They were called North Carolina and South Carolina. Each colony could have a general assembly. The king said that some settlers in the Carolinas could vote for the members of their general assembly.

The king sent governors to North Carolina and South Carolina. The governor of each colony could tell the General Assembly that its laws were wrong. The settlers in the Carolinas had to pay taxes to the General Assemblies and to the king of England.

Georgia

In the early 1700s, the king of England had many colonies in America. But he thought that more English people should live in his southern colonies. He wanted strong colonies on the southern part of America.

The king of Spain also had many colonies in America. Most Spanish colonies were not near the English colonies. But one colony was south of the Carolinas. Today, this land is called Florida. The king of Spain had an army in Florida.

The king of England was afraid that the Spanish army might fight against the settlers in the Carolinas. He decided to make another colony between the Carolinas and the Spanish colony. Today, this land is called Georgia.

In 1732, the king of England gave a charter to James Oglethorpe. The king gave him the land south of the Carolinas and north of Florida. The charter said that Oglethorpe could own this land for 20 years. After 20 years, Georgia would become a royal colony.

Oglethorpe wanted to help some people in England. These people had trouble in England. Some of them owed money to people and could not pay it back. So the government had put them in jail. Oglethorpe thought that these people could make a good life in his colony. Other people did not want to go to the king's church. They wanted to go to different churches. Oglethorpe said that they could go to their own churches in Georgia.

James Oglethorpe started the colony of Georgia.

Oglethorpe took some of these people to Georgia. He paid for their trip and gave them land, seeds, and tools. The settlers built farms in Georgia. Oglethorpe made the laws for the colony. He told the settlers that they could not make their own laws. He also said that the settlers could not own slaves in Georgia. In 1751, Oglethrope thought that the settlers needed more workers. So he said that the settlers could own slaves in Georgia. In 1752, Georgia became a royal colony.

Life in the Southern Colonies

The settlers in the middle colonies and the New England colonies had small farms. They did not need many workers on these farms. So they had only a few slaves.

The settlers in the southern colonies had larger farms. They needed many workers. They had slaves to help them on their farms. Some people in the South did not think that it was right to own slaves. Other settlers owned many slaves.

In the New England colonies, it was hard to grow a lot of food. There were many rocks in the land. The settlers could grow only enough food for themselves. So they did not sell any food to merchants in England. The land in the southern colonies was very good. The settlers grew a lot of tobacco, cotton, and rice. So they sold these things to merchants in England.

CHAPTER 6

The Colonies in the Middle 1700s

Africans in America

In the middle of the 1700s, many white people lived in the colonies. Some of these colonists were born in the colonies. Their families had lived in the colonies for many years. Other people were born in Europe. They came to live in the colonies. They also became colonists.

Many black people lived in the colonies. Some of these black people were born in Africa. They did not want to come to America. But some sailors had made them come to the colonies. They had to live in the colonies. They could not go back to Africa.

Owners made their slaves work hard.

Most Africans in America were slaves. The colonists owned them. They told the slaves what to do. They did not pay the slaves for their work. The slaves could not marry white people. The children of these Africans were also slaves. Most of them could not go to school.

Africans were different from the Europeans and the colonists. Africans did not live like the Europeans or the colonists. The Europeans and the colonists thought that they were better than the Africans. They also thought that they had the only right way of life. In the colonies, the Africans could not live like the people in Africa.

Africans did not have the same kinds of religions as the Europeans and the colonists. In the colonies, some Africans learned about the religion of the colonists. The colonists let some slaves go to their churches. But in some churches, the Africans had to sit in the back of the church.

There were only a few slaves in the New England colonies and the middle colonies. The farmers in these colonies did not need a lot of workers. Some slaves did other kinds of work for their owners. They did not work on farms.

The slaves and the colonists had many fights. After each fight, the colonists still owned the slaves. But some colonists thought that people could own slaves. Other colonists thought that people should not own other people.

Sometimes, owners told their slaves that they could go free. Other times, the slaves had to work for a while. The owners paid these slaves for this work. These slaves could pay some money to their owners.

Then the owners let them go free. The free Africans could buy some land. But they could not vote for members of the general assembly.

The farms were very big in the southern colonies. The colonists needed a lot of slaves. Some colonists were not nice to their slaves. But all slave owners made their slaves work very hard. Slaves could not do what they wanted to do. They could not move away from the farms of their owners.

In the southern colonies, some colonists were afraid that the slaves would try to fight against their owner. These colonists made laws about slaves. Some laws said that colonists could own slaves. Slaves could not run away from their owners.

Other laws said that slaves did not have any rights. Slaves could not have meetings. They could not marry white people.

Slaves had to obey all the laws of the colonies. If they did not, their owners could hit them or even kill them. The Africans could not have a trial. Only the white colonists could have a trial in the southern colonies.

The First Americans

The colonists also thought that they were better than the first Americans. They did not understand the first Americans. They thought that the first Americans did not live in the right way.

The first Americans did not think that people should own land. They thought that their gods owned all the land. The first Americans thought that people should not hurt the land or the water. The first Americans did not cut down so many trees.

The colonists cut down a lot of trees and built big towns. These towns and farms got bigger. Then the first Americans got angry. They thought that the colonists were hurting the land. The first Americans and the colonists fought about the land many times.

The colonists traded with the first Americans.

At first, the colonists did not know how to grow things on the land in America. But the first Americans knew how to grow many kinds of foods. Some of these foods did not grow in Europe. So first Americans showed the colonists how to grow these things. They also showed the colonists how to make a special kind of boat. Then the colonists could travel on the rivers.

At first, the colonists thought that the first Americans did not know how to fight well. In Europe, soldiers fought together in a line. The first Americans hid behind trees. Then they could surprise people and kill them. After a while, the colonists decided that the first Americans knew a better way to fight.

Some colonists thought that the first Americans

should be their slaves. But the first Americans did not want to be slaves. They fought against the colonists. They moved to other land in America. Only a few first Americans became slaves of the colonists.

The colonists thought that the religions of the first Americans were wrong. Some colonists told the first Americans all about their religions. These colonists wanted the first Americans to go to their kinds of church.

Many tribes of first Americans lived near the New England colonies. One of the tribes was the Iroquois. Another tribe was the Algonquins. The Iroquois fought against the Algonquins. Sometimes, the Iroquois also fought against the French settlers.

In 1675, the Iroquois and other tribes started a confederation. Together, they would have a strong army. They fought against the English settlers and the Algonquins. Many people died in these fights.

The English settlers won most of the fights against these first Americans. They kept the land of the first Americans. Later, the Iroquois and the confederation became friends of the English settlers.

Religion

In the 1600s and 1700s, most countries in Europe had their own church. All people in a country had to go to the church of that country. All people had to have the same religion. But some people did not want this religion. They got into trouble.

In Europe, the church was often part of the government. The same people made the laws for the church and the government. These people decided that everyone had to pay taxes to the church of their country. If they did not, they had to go to jail.

Colonists went to church in the New England colonies.

Some people came to America because they wanted to have their own religions. These people started colonies. Some colonies had a church for the colony. The colonists had trouble if they wanted their own religion. The same people made the laws for the church and the government of these colonies. All of the people had to pay taxes to the government. Then the government gave money to the church of these colonies.

In other colonies, the government said that the people did not have to go to the church of the colony. Some people in these colonies made laws for the government. Other people made all of the laws for the churches.

In 1649, the General Assembly of Maryland made a law about religion. This law said that the people in Maryland had to pray to Jesus Christ. But they could pray in any kind of church. Jews do not pray to Jesus Christ. The law did not help them. They wanted to have their own religion. So they still had trouble in Maryland.

In 1701, the General Assembly of Pennsylvania made a law about religion. This law said that people could go to many different kinds of churches. But all people had to think that there was one god. The law also said that all voters had to pray to Jesus Christ. Jews could not vote in Pennsylvania.

In the 1700s, each colony wanted more people in it. In big colonies, more people could have jobs and get richer. In many colonies, the government decided that the colonists could have different religions. They had many different religions. They did not have to be members of the church of the colony. But the government of the colony gave some money to that church. Some settlers did not want any of their tax money to go to the church of the colony. So they did not want to pay their taxes. Sometimes, the government put them in jail.

By the middle of the 1700s, people in each colony had different religions. But some general assemblies said that only members of the church of the colony could vote. Later, some general assemblies changed this law. Then more men could vote. They could also be members of the general assemblies. Then the church of the colony did not have so much power in the government anymore.

Schools

In the 1600s and the 1700s, many colonists wanted their children to read, write, and use numbers. They wanted their children to read the Bible. They wanted their sons to get better in their jobs. They wanted their daughters to know how to take care of their homes.

Some boys went to school for many years. Most girls only went to school for a few years. Some children never went to school.

In the New England colonies, the colonists wanted all of their children to go to school. In 1647, the Massachusetts Bay Colony made a law about schools. Each big town had to start a school for children. The rich people in the town had to pay a lot of taxes for the school. The poor people in the town did not have to pay these taxes. All children could go to the school. Other colonies in New England also made laws about schools.

In the southern colonies, teachers came to the homes of rich children. In the southern and middle colonies, there were only a few schools. Most of these schools were part of a church in the colony.

Most African children could not go to school. They did not have teachers. Most of them did not learn how to read and write.

Women had many different jobs at home.

Women

Women in the colonies took care of children and older people. Some women worked hard on the farms. They helped grow food. They cooked and made clothes for their family. Stores did not sell clothes. They only sold cloth.

Sometimes, women made other things at home. They sold them to other people. But they had to give the money to the men in their families.

In the 1600s and 1700s, most women did not work outside of their homes. Men did not think that women needed to learn many things. Some girls never went to school. Most girls did not go to school for many years. They could not become doctors or lawyers.

The men in the general assemblies made laws about women. Women could not vote. They could not become members of the general assemblies. Women could not own land. The men in the families kept all of the money.

John Peter Zenger

In 1733, there were no televisions or radios anywhere in the world. But people could read a newspaper. In the colonies, newspapers were not very big. Each week, the colonists could buy a new newspaper. Today, there are many different kinds of newspapers. They have many pages. People can buy a new newspaper every day.

In 1733, John Peter Zenger started a newspaper in New York. In the colonies and England, there was a law about newspapers. This law said that writers could not speak against the government in newspapers. The colonists had to obey this law.

The colony of New York had a trial for John Peter Zenger.

In New York, the governor wanted the colonists to pay a lot of taxes. He kept some of the tax money for himself. In 1734, Zenger's newspaper said that the governor was wrong. The governor got angry. He said that Zenger had broken the law. The governor made Zenger go to jail.

The laws in the colony said that the government could not keep people in jail without a trial. After ten months in jail, Zenger had a trial. At the trial, other colonists would decide if Zenger was right or wrong.

At the trial, Zenger said that he had broken the law about newspapers. But he also said that the newspaper had told the truth. The men at the trial said that Zenger was right. After 1735, newspapers in the colonies could speak against the government if they told the truth.

CHAPTER 7

The Seven Years' War

New France

In the early 1600s, French and English explorers had landed in America. By the middle of the 1600s, England had many colonies in America. The king of France thought that it owned the land north of the English colonies. Today, this land is called Canada.

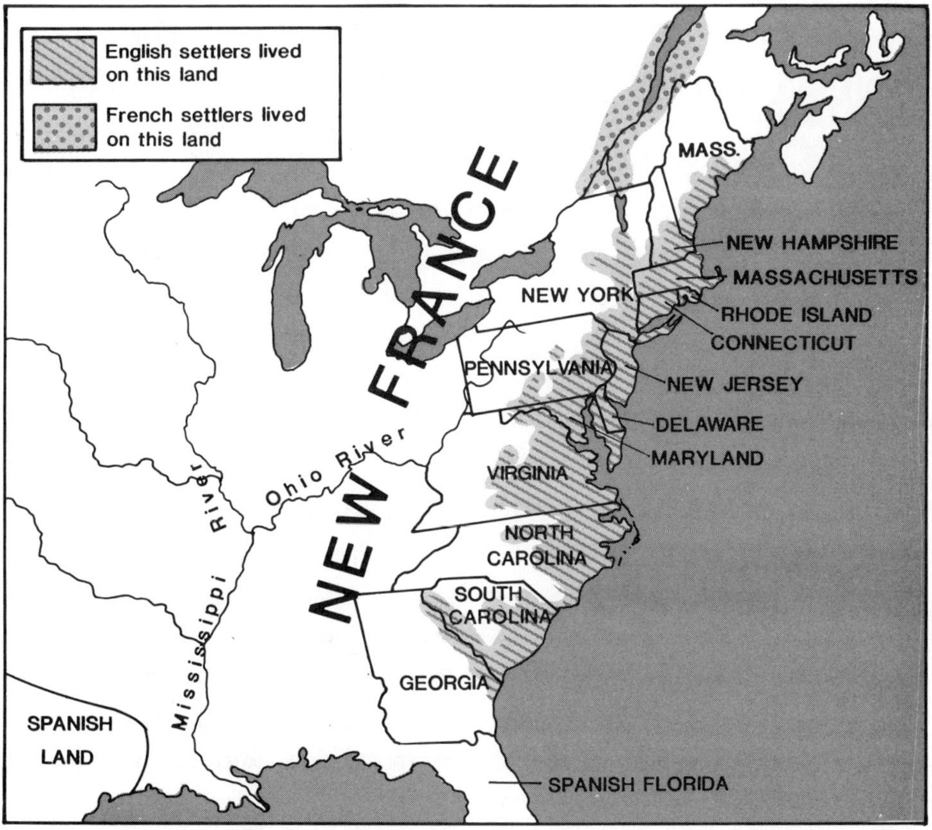

New France and the English Colonies

In 1673, the king of France wanted to own more land in America. So he sent some explorers to North America. These explorers sailed on big rivers. These rivers were the Mississippi River, the Ohio River, and the Arkansas River. Some explorers also sailed on some big lakes. These lakes were northwest of the English colonies. Today, they are called the Great Lakes.

After 1682, the king of France thought that he owned all the land around these rivers and the Great Lakes. This land was west of the English colonies. All the French land in America was called New France. Part of this land was called Louisiana. Louisiana was west of the Mississippi River.

In the early 1700s, French settlers built towns and small farms in the northern part of New France. The farms and towns were near the St. Lawrence River. The towns were called Quebec and Montreal. But the French settlers in Louisiana did not build farms or towns. They were fur traders. They traded with the first Americans. They gave blankets and guns to the men in the tribes. The first Americans gave them furs. Then the French fur traders sold the furs to merchants in France.

The French settlers also built a town in the southern part of New France. It was called New Orleans. It was near the Mississippi River.

The French settlers were Catholics. Some of them thought that the first Americans should also be Catholics. Some of these settlers tried to teach the first Americans about their religion. But most first Americans did not want to become Catholics. They wanted to pray in their own way.

All of New France was one royal colony. Not

French settlers made friends with the Algonquins.

very many colonists lived there. The king of France made all the laws for the colonists in New France. There was no general assembly.

Many different tribes of first Americans lived in New France. One tribe was the Algonquins. Some Algonquins became friends with the French fur traders. They traded with each other. The Algonquins knew that the French fur traders did not build many farms or towns. The French fur traders were not taking all the land in New France.

Some first Americans were not friends with the French fur traders. These first Americans were the Iroquois. The king of France sent an army to New France. This army fought against the Iroquois and some other first Americans. The French army also fought against English settlers.

The Seven Years' War in America

In the early 1700s, England, France, and Spain were fighting all over the world. They fought about the land in their colonies. Each country had colonies in many parts of the world. Each country wanted to have the most colonies. England had many colonies on the east coast of America. There were many English settlers in America.

The king of England thought that only English ships should trade in English colonies. The king of France and the king of Spain thought that their ships should be able to trade in the English colonies, too. The French army and navy fought against the English army and navy. The king of Spain decided to help the king of France. But only England and France fought about the land in America.

In 1753, the king of England said that some English settlers could own land in the royal colonies. Some settlers in Virginia moved to land west of Virginia. It was part of the land in the colony of Virginia. Today, this land is called the Ohio Valley.

But the king of France also thought that he owned this land. So the French government built forts along the Ohio River. The French army lived in these forts. It tried to keep the English settlers out of the Ohio Valley. The French army wanted to keep this land for the king of France.

The governor of Virginia sent some soldiers to the Ohio Valley. One soldier was George Washington. Washington told the French army that England owned this land. He told the French soldiers to leave the Ohio Valley. But the French army did not listen to him.

In 1754, Washington and the English soldiers built a fort in the Ohio Valley. This English fort was near a French fort. The French soldiers fought against the English soldiers at the English fort. The Algonquins helped the French army. The Algonquins did not want so many English settlers to live on their land. Washington and the English soldiers lost this fight.

The French forts and the English fort were near the colonies of New York and Pennsylvania. The settlers in those colonies were afraid of the French army and the Algonquins. But they had made friends with the Iroquois and their confederation. This confederation was strong.

This English fort was in the Ohio Valley.

Some English colonists wanted to fight against the French army and settlers in New France. They did not want French settlers to take the land in the Ohio Valley. They decided that their general assemblies could try to work together.

In 1754, some men from different colonies met in Albany, New York. They talked about the first Americans and the land in the colonies. They also met with some men from the confederation of first Americans.

Benjamin Franklin was one of the men at this meeting. He wanted the English colonies to have one government. This new government would be a confederation. It could talk about trouble in the colonies. The confederation could have one army. This army could fight against the French army. But other men did not think the same way. They thought that the government of each colony should be strong. They did not want one strong government for all the colonies. The men at this meeting decided that the colonies would not start a confederation.

After this meeting, the army of England came to America. Then the English colonists and the army from England started to fight against the French army and the Algonquins.

The French army had been in America for a long time. The Algonquins had taught them how to fight in the woods.

The English colonists also knew how to fight in the woods. But they had to listen to the general of the army from England. The general told the soldiers what to do. But he did not know how to fight in the woods. He told the English soldiers and colonists to march in a line in fights. He also told them to wear red coats in the fights. The French army and the Algonquins could see these coats in the woods. Then it was easy to kill the English soldiers and colonists. So the English soldiers and colonists lost many fights.

In 1756, the English king sent a new general to America. Sometimes, this general listened to the colonists. Then the colonists and the English army started to win some fights. They took over some of the French forts.

Many people died in the Seven Years' War.

For seven years, the French army and the Algonquins fought against the English soldiers and colonists in America. Some first Americans helped the colonists. The French army and navy also fought against the English army and navy in other parts of the world.

In 1763, England won the war. The kings of England, France, and Spain wrote a special paper. This paper is called a treaty. A treaty says what each country will do. This treaty said many things. The king of France had to give a lot of his land to the kings of England and Spain. Spain had helped France in the war. So the king of France gave Louisiana to the king of Spain. The king of France had to give the rest of New France to the king of England. The king of Spain also had to give Florida to the king of England.

After the Seven Years' War, the king of England owned a lot more land in America. This new land was between the English colonies and the Mississippi River and north of the New England colonies.

After the war, the English colonists felt good. They could move west. They were not afraid of the French army or the Algonquins anymore. They knew that they could win a war against these people. They also had learned a lot about the English army. The English colonists knew that they were better soldiers than the soldiers in the army from England.

CHAPTER 8

English Colonies in America

Trade between England and the Colonies

In the 1600s, some countries in Europe had many colonies in the world. These countries had wars about their colonies. Each country wanted to own the most land in the world. The king of each country thought that a country with many colonies would be rich and strong. Each king thought that colonists could send things back from his colonies. He also thought that colonists could buy things from the merchants in his country. Then the merchants and the country would become richer.

In the 1600s, the government of England owned many colonies in America. It thought that the colonies could make England rich. In 1651, the government of England made laws about ships. These laws said that only English ships could go to the English colonies and bring things back to England.

In 1663, the government of England made new laws about trade in the colonies. One law said that the English colonists could trade only with merchants from England. They could not buy things from other countries or colonies of other countries. Things from other countries are called imports. Only the merchants from England could buy things from other countries. Then they could sell them to the colonists. Taxes on imports made things cost even more money. But the colonists had to pay taxes on imports.

Another law said that the colonists could not sell their things right to merchants in other countries. Ships with things from the colonies had to go to England or other English colonies. Then they could go to another country. People sell things to merchants in other countries. These things are called exports. The merchants in other countries could buy exports from the English colonies. But they had to pay taxes on these exports.

The colonists did not like these laws. They knew that things from other countries cost less money than things from England. But the law said that they could not buy things from other countries. The taxes on exports would make things from the English colonies cost a lot of money. So people in other countries would not buy exports from the colonies. Most of the time, colonists did not obey these laws.

The governors of the colonies could not always make sure that the colonists obeyed the laws about trade. Often, the colonists traded with people in other countries and their colonies. But the governors did not make most of these colonists go to jail.

The colonists bought molasses from the colonies in the West Indies. These colonies were islands south of Florida. Some of the West Indies were English colonies. Other islands in the West Indies were Spanish and French colonies.

In 1733, Parliament made a law about molasses. This law said that the colonists had to pay a tax on molasses from the Spanish and French colonies in the West Indies. But the colonists broke the laws of Parliament. Sometimes, they bought molasses from the French and Spanish colonies. Then they did not pay a tax on it. Other times, they bought molasses

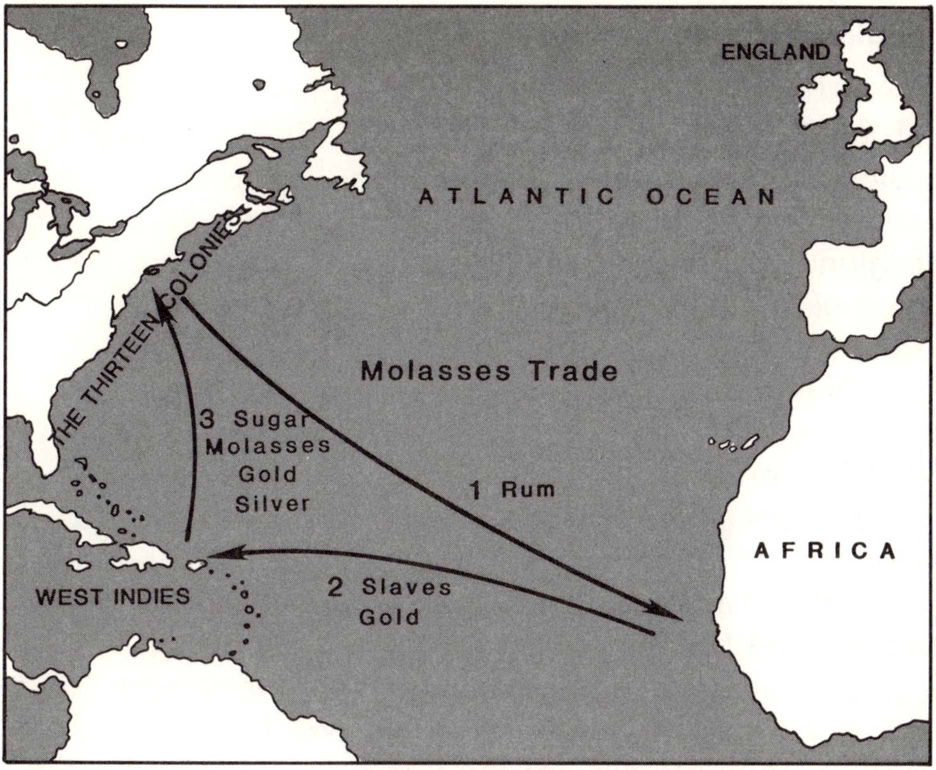

The Molasses Trade

from the English colonies.

Colonists made rum out of molasses. They sold the rum to other colonists. These colonists were ship owners or merchants. They took the rum to Africa and sold it to the Africans. In Africa, they bought slaves and took them to the West Indies. In the West Indies, they sold some of the slaves and bought sugar and molasses. Then they took these things and some slaves back to the colonies.

For a long time, the colonists did not obey the laws about imports and exports. The English government knew that the colonists traded in Africa and in the West Indies. But they did not make the colonists obey the laws about trade.

England Needs Money

After the Seven Years' War, England owned a lot of land in Asia and North America. There were colonies in many parts of this land. England was rich and strong because of all of these colonies. But England had spent a lot of money on the wars. The king of England thought that the English colonists should help pay for the war in North America.

England also wanted to keep its new land and colonies safe. The king of England wanted to keep soldiers in all of the English colonies. They would try to keep the colonies safe. In all parts of the world, the soldiers from England fought against other people. In North America, soldiers from England had to fight against the first Americans and other Europeans.

The king of England thought that the English colonists in North America should pay for his army. But the colonists did not think that they needed the army from England. They thought that they could fight for themselves.

The king of England also had to pay the governor of each colony. Some other English men helped the governor. England had to pay these men, too. But the colonists did not think that they needed the governor and these men.

The king of England wanted more tax money from the English colonists. This money could pay for the English government and soldiers in North America. The king of England also wanted the merchants in England to get richer. Then England would get richer. So the king of England made more laws about taxes for the colonies.

Land

Before the Seven Years' War, most colonists lived on the land between the Atlantic Ocean and the Appalachian Mountains. They had charters from England for this land. They thought that they could tell the first Americans to move. Sometimes, the first Americans moved west. Other times, they fought against the colonists.

Before the Seven Years' War, the king of France thought that he owned the land between the Appalachian Mountains and the Mississippi River. This land was west of the English colonies. The English colonists did not have charters for this land. But some of them moved there anyway. They built houses and farms. They did not have their own governments in this land. Sometimes, they fought against the first Americans.

After the Seven Years' War, the king of England owned this land. Parliament told the colonists to make friends with the first Americans on this land. Parliament wanted the English merchants to trade with these first Americans. Parliament did not want the colonists and the first Americans to fight about this land.

After the Seven Years' War, Parliament and the general assemblies in the colonies had fights about the land west of the colonies. Colonists sent men to talk to the members of Parliament. Some of these colonists said that only fur traders should go to the new land. They did not think that more colonists should live there. Other colonists told members of Parliament that the colonists should make new colonies on this land.

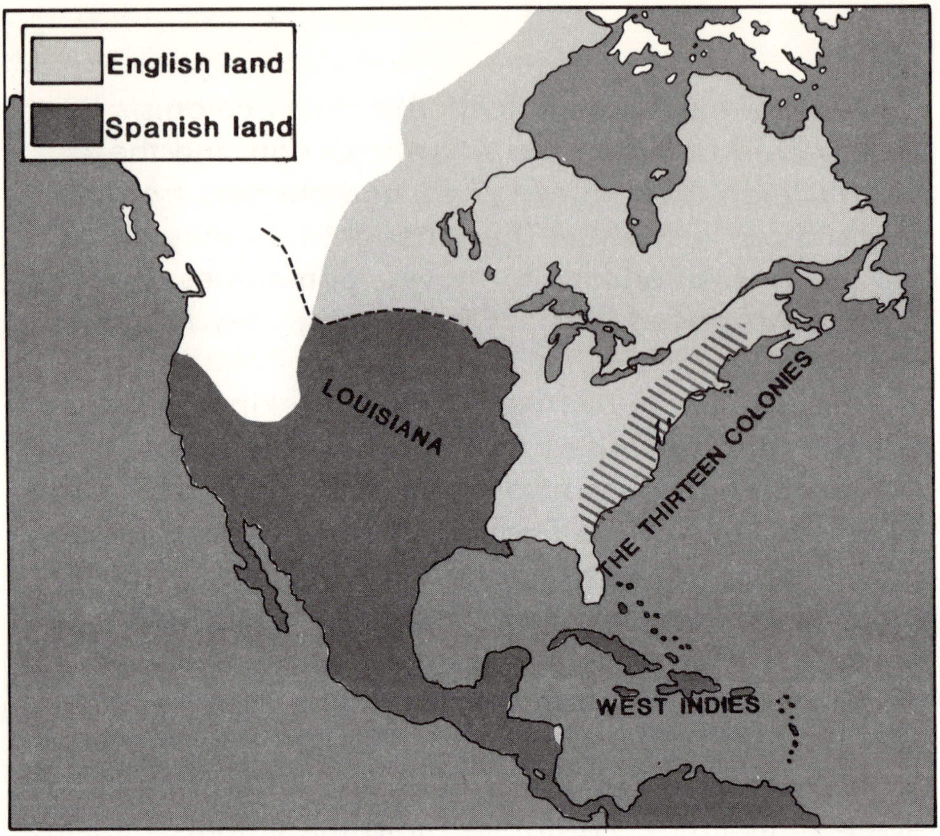

North America in 1763

After the Seven Years' War, Parliament said that the colonists could not live on the new land. But the colonists did not always obey the laws of Parliament. They knew that Parliament could not keep them out of this land. The general assemblies said that the colonists could move to this land. More colonists moved there. The colonists and the first Americans fought about this land.

After the Seven Years' War, the king of England thought that he owned a lot of land in North America. The government of England made the laws for all the colonies. But more than half of the settlers on English land had not come from England. The settlers in Florida had come from Spain. Many of the settlers in Canada had come from France. Some settlers in the English colonies had come from other European countries. These settlers did not always want to obey the laws of Parliament.

Money

The government of each country makes the coins and paper money for that country. Merchants and other people in the country use this money. In 1764, the English colonists used the coins and paper money of England. The Spanish colonists used the coins and paper money of Spain. The French colonists used French money. None of the colonies had their own coins. So the colonists used French, Spanish, and English coins.

For many years, the English colonists had been trading with the Spanish and French colonists in the West Indies. They had trouble with the different coins and paper money. So the English colonies started to make their own paper money. They used this money in the other English colonies and in the West Indies. But Parliament did not want the English colonies to make their own money.

Parliament thought that only countries should have their own money. Colonies were not countries. Parliament was afraid that the colonies were getting too strong. Parliament wanted to make sure that there was only one government for England and the English colonies. In 1764, Parliament made a new law about money in the colonies. The law said that the colonists could not make their own paper money. The colonists had to pay their taxes with the money of England.

The colonists bought some things from merchants in England. They had to pay for these things with English coins and paper money. After 1764, the colonists did not buy and sell so many things in England. Then they did not have a lot of English coins and paper money. But the merchants in the colonies needed English coins and paper money to pay taxes on imports. They could not use the paper money of the colony to pay these taxes to England.

CHAPTER 9

The English Colonists Start to Fight

New Laws for the Colonies

After the Seven Years' War, Parliament decided that the colonies should help to pay for the English army and navy. So it said that the colonists should obey the laws about taxes on imports and exports. Parliament sent some men to the colonies. These men had to make sure that the governor of each colony got these taxes from the colonists.

In 1764, Parliament made a new law about taxes. It said that the colonists had to pay more taxes on some imports. These taxes made imports cost a lot of money. The colonists did not want to pay these taxes. The English army and navy tried to make the colonists pay these taxes. The colonists got angry. They did not think that Parliament should make laws about taxes in the colonies. They thought that their own governments should make laws about taxes in their colonies.

In 1765, Parliament made another law for the colonies. This law said that soldiers from England could live in the houses of the colonists. The soldiers did not have to pay rent to the colonists. The colonies had to pay for food and clothes for these English soldiers. The colonists did not like this law.

In 1765, Parliament also made another new law about taxes. This law was called the Stamp Act.

It said that the colonists had to buy stamps from England. They had to put these stamps on all kinds of papers. Some of these papers showed that someone owned a house, a farm, or land. Other papers were about money from banks. Other papers were newspapers and papers for churches.

The colonists did not like the new English laws. Merchants paid the taxes on imports. The merchants added the taxes to the cost of the imports. The colonists did not have to buy these things. Sometimes, they bought them and even forgot about these taxes. But the colonists could not forget about the stamp tax. They had to use these papers. So they had to buy stamps for them from the government of England. All of the money from the stamp tax went to Parliament.

The colonists were angry about the Stamp Act.

The Sons of Liberty burned down buildings.

Some men in the colonies got together. They called themselves the Sons of Liberty. They decided to burn the stamps. They also burned down some English buildings. There were stamps in these buildings. The Sons of Liberty had many fights against the English army in the colonies.

Many general assemblies decided that the colonists should not have to obey the Stamp Act. In 1765, nine colonies sent representatives to a meeting in New York. This meeting was called the Stamp Act Congress. The men at this meeting said that the colonists had to obey all the laws of the general assemblies. The general assemblies would make their own laws about taxes. The general assemblies would decide if the colonists had to obey all of the laws of Parliament.

The Stamp Act Congress decided that the colonists did not have to use the stamps. None of the colonists ever bought the stamps. The Stamp Act Congress also decided that the merchants in the colonies would not buy so many things from England. They could buy more things from the French and Spanish colonies in the West Indies. They could also buy things from people in the other English colonies.

Most colonists listened to the Stamp Act Congress. They did not buy things from England. Then the merchants in England had trouble. They could not sell so many things to the English colonists. The merchants in England did not make so much money anymore. The merchants in the colonies also had trouble. They did not trade with the merchants in England. So they did not have a lot of English coins and paper money. But they needed this money to pay the taxes on the imports.

By 1766, the merchants in England were upset. They told Parliament that they did not like the Stamp Act. Many other people in England also told Parliament that the colonists should not have to obey the Stamp Act. After a while, Parliament changed the Stamp Act. The new law said that the colonists did not have to buy the special stamps anymore.

In 1767, Parliament decided that the colonists in America should pay more taxes. So Parliament made new laws. These laws were called the Townshend Acts. These laws said that the colonists had to pay taxes on some imports from England. Some of these imports were tea, lead, and glass. The colonists needed these things. They could not get them in the colonies. They had to buy them from England.

Parliament knew that some of the colonists would not obey the Townshend Acts. So one part of the Townshend Acts said that people from the English government could go into the house of any colonist. These people could look for imports. They did not have to say what they were looking for. They could just look at everything in the house. If the colonist had not paid the tax on an import, they could make the colonist go to court.

The colonists did not want people from the English government to go into their houses. The colonists got very angry about the Townshend Acts. Many colonists would not buy things from England. They wrote letters to Parliament and to people in England. The general assemblies wrote letters to Parliament, too.

The First Big Fights against England

In 1770, there were soldiers from England in the colonies. The colonists and these soldiers had many fights. One big fight was in Boston. Boston was a town in the Massachusetts colony. Some colonists died in this fight.

One of these colonists was Crispus Attucks. Attucks had been a slave. He had run away from his owner. By 1770, he had been working in Massachusetts for a long time. He was not a slave anymore. But he did not have the same rights as the other colonists. He could not vote for the members of the General Assembly. Attucks wanted to fight against the laws of Parliament. He died in the fight in Boston.

English soldiers killed Crispus Attucks.

After this fight, the colonists were angry at the army from England. They did not want the English soldiers in their homes. They wanted these soldiers to leave Boston. They did not want the army from England to kill any other colonists. In Boston, they had a trial for some soldiers from England. Two of these soldiers had to go to jail.

After the fight in Boston, Parliament changed some laws. One new law said that the colonists did not have to let the soldiers from England live in their houses. Another new law said that the colonists had to pay taxes only on tea from England. Parliament wanted the colonists to know that they still had to pay taxes to England. But they did not have to pay taxes on so many things.

For a little while, there were not many fights in the colonies. Many colonists were glad. They did not like to fight against England. But many colonists were still angry. The colonists in Massachusetts wrote letters to the colonists in other colonies. These letters told the other colonists what was going on in Massachusetts.

The government of each colony was not very strong. Some colonists thought that the colonies needed one government for all the colonies. Other colonists did not want one government for all the colonies. England had one strong government. So some colonists were afraid of a strong government.

The British East India Company was a big English company. It sold tea all over the world. But in 1773, it had trouble. The colonists in America had not bought much tea from it for a long time. The company was not making very much money anymore. The company asked Parliament for help.

The British East India Company needed some money. So Parliament made a law. It said that the company could borrow some money from Parliament. The company had to pay this money back. Parliament also said that the company could sell its tea to the colonists for very little money. Parliament wanted the colonists to buy tea from the British East India

Company. It did not want the colonists to buy tea from other countries or colonies.

In 1773, Parliament also made another law about tea. This law was called the Tea Act. It said that the British East India Company did not have to sell tea to the merchants in England. They could sell it to special merchants in the colonies. The colonists still had to pay a tax on tea. But the tea would cost less money than tea from other places. Some colonists were very angry. They did not want any colonists to pay taxes to England.

In the colonies, there were many fights about the Tea Act. Some colonists did not want ships from the British East India Company to come into the colonies. In Boston, some colonists dressed up like first Americans. They got on a ship from the British East India Company. Then they threw the tea into the water.

Colonists threw tea from an English ship in Boston.

Parliament got angry at these colonists. It did not want any more fights in the colonies. In 1774, Parliament made some new laws. One law said that ships could not go to Boston anymore. Another law said that the colonists in Massachusetts could not have town meetings anymore. Another law said that the colonists could not have trials for people from the government of England. Trials for these people would be in England. Parliament also sent more soldiers to Massachusetts.

Some colonists were very angry about these new laws. In September 1774, they had a big meeting in Philadelphia, Pennsylvania. This meeting was called the First Continental Congress. Representatives from most of the 13 colonies came to this meeting. Georgia did not send any representatives.

At the meeting, the representatives talked about England and the colonies. They also decided that the colonies would all help each other. They decided to talk to the merchants in their colonies. They did not think that the merchants should trade with England. They decided that they would meet again in a few months.

Some colonists thought that England should still own the colonies. The king of England should still make laws for them. These people were called Loyalists. Other colonists thought that England should not make laws for the colonies. These people were called Patriots. They did not want the army from England in the colonies. They wanted to be ready for a fight against the army from England.

On April 18, 1775, the Patriots had their first big fights against the army from England. These fights were at Lexington and at Concord. Lexington and Concord were towns near Boston. There were also other fights in the New England colonies.

Colonists fought against English soldiers in Lexington, Massachusetts.

On May 10, 1775, the Continental Congress met again. This meeting was called the Second Continental Congress. Some representatives at this meeting thought that England should not own the colonies. They thought that the colonies should have their independence from England. They wanted their own governments in the colonies. These governments would make all the laws for the colonies. The colonists would not have to obey the laws of Parliament anymore.

Other representatives at the meeting did not want independence from England. But they did not want to pay so much tax money to England. They did not want anyone to come into their houses and look for things.

At last, the Second Continental Congress said that each colony should start its own government. This new government would make all the laws for its colony. Then the colony would become a state.

The Second Continental Congress also said that the colonies needed an army. This army would fight against the army from England. It would fight for all the colonies. The representatives also wanted Parliament to change the laws about the colonies. If it did not, the army would fight against the army from England. The representatives decided that George Washington would be the general of the army. This army would be called the Continental Army.

In June 1775, the Patriots fought against the army from England. Many Patriots and soldiers from England died in this fight near Boston. The king of England was very upset. He did not think that the colonies were so strong. The king sent the English navy to the colonies. These ships would not let other ships go into the colonies. The king also sent more soldiers. The colonists and the soldiers from England fought for a long time.

After a while, the Second Continental Congress decided to send some men to Europe. These men would ask the governments of other countries for help. Some of the governments wanted to help the colonies. France and Spain said that they might help the colonies.

In 1776, the colonists and the soldiers from England were still fighting. Most of the fights were in the northern colonies. A few fights were in the southern colonies. The Patriots were able to win many fights.

George Washington won another fight near Boston. Then the army and navy from England thought that they could not win in Boston. So they left Boston. The English ships took some soldiers and Loyalists back to England. Many Loyalists did not want to stay in the colonies anymore. They were afraid of the fights against the army from England.

The Patriots and the Loyalists did not think the same way about the colonies. They had many fights with each other. Some Patriots started to write things about the fights against England.

CHAPTER 10

The Revolution

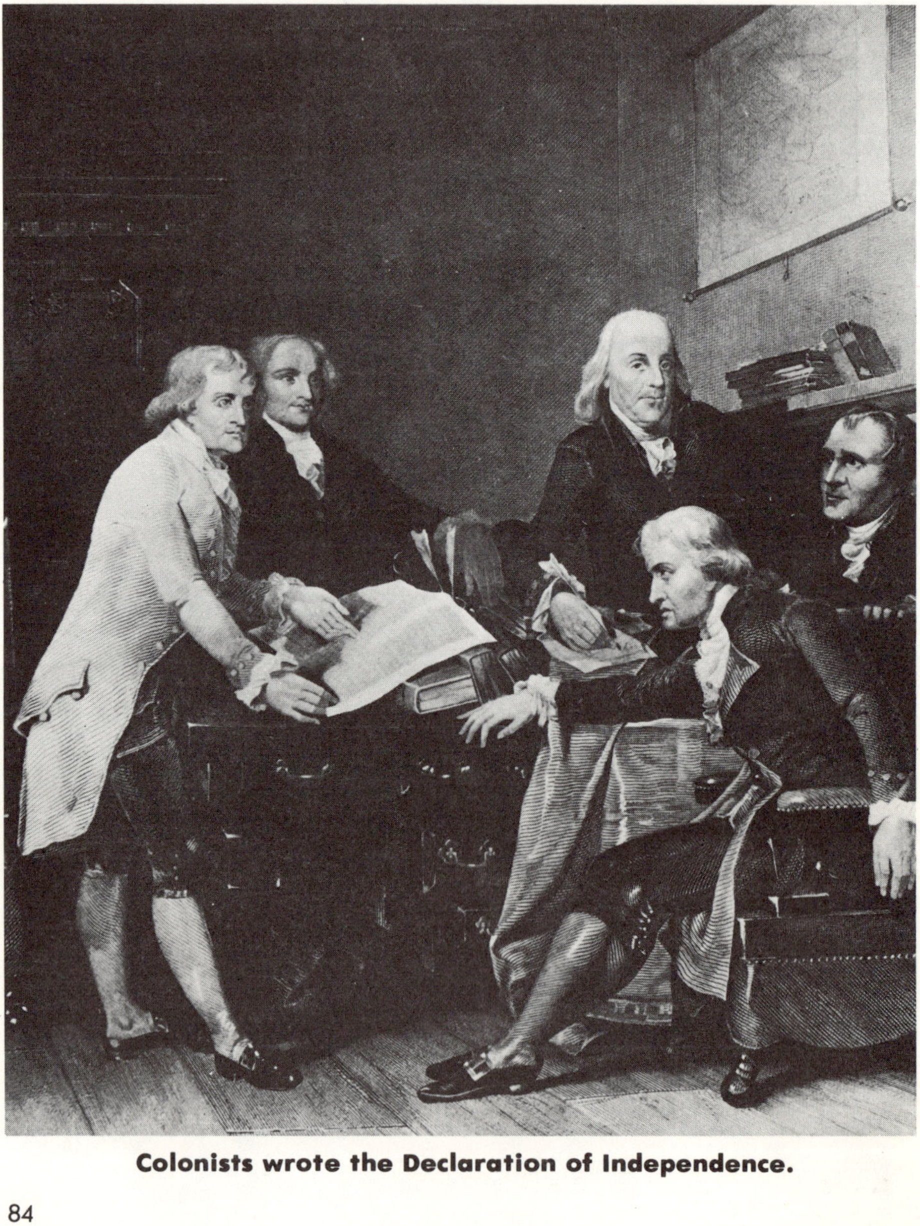

Colonists wrote the Declaration of Independence.

The Declaration of Independence

On July 4, 1776, the Second Continental Congress decided that the 13 colonies should not be part of England anymore. The colonists did not want to obey the laws of England. They wanted more rights. So the Second Continental Congress wrote a special paper. It is called the Declaration of Independence.

The Declaration of Independence told about the fights between the colonists and England. It said that the colonists did not want England to own the colonies anymore. They wanted their independence from England. They wanted to make their own laws. The Declaration of Independence also talked about government and rights in the colonies. The members of the Second Continental Congress wrote their names on the Declaration of Independence. They sent it to the king of England. It took a long time to get to England.

The colonists would have to fight for their independence. They would have to fight against England. This kind of war is called a revolution.

The Second Continental Congress talked about a government for the colonies. The colonists did not have one government for all the colonies. The Continental Congress could not tell the colonists what to do. It also talked about the Continental Army. It could tell the army what to do. But colonists did not have to be soldiers in the Continental Army. Colonists did not have to pay any taxes to this Continental Congress. The congress could only ask the colonies to send men and money for the army.

The Colonists Fight against England

George Washington was the general of the Continental Army. He did not have enough soldiers in his army. At first, he said that no slaves or free Africans could be in his army. Some colonists thought that he was right. They did not think that any African should have a gun. They were afraid that slaves might shoot their owners or other colonists.

Members of the Continental Congress knew that many Loyalists could send their slaves to fight against the Continental Army. Then the English Army would have more soldiers. Some members of the Continental Congress thought that slaves could be soldiers in the Continental Army. But other members still thought that slaves should not fight for their owners.

After a while, Washington decided to let Africans become soldiers in the Continental Army. The Continental Congress said that slaves could be soldiers. After the war, these black soldiers would be free. But after the war, many black soldiers still had to be slaves.

After July 4, 1776, more colonists became soldiers in the Continental Army. The soldiers came from many colonies. But most colonists did not become soldiers. The Continental Army was still small. The English army had many more soldiers. The Continental Congress had some ships, but they did not have a navy.

The government of England had an army and a strong navy. It was hard for the colonists to fight against the English navy. But most of the fights in the Revolution were on land. The soldiers from England did not know how to fight in the woods. They did not know about the land in the colonies. The colonists were fighting on their own land. They knew about this land.

The English army had other troubles. The English army had to get its food and guns from England. English ships brought these things to the cities on the Atlantic coast. Then the English army had to take them into the woods for the other English soldiers. The colonists did not want the English army to get the food and guns to the other soldiers. So the colonists fought against the English soldiers near the coast.

At first, Washington and the Continental Army fought against the English army in New York and New Jersey. In October 1777, the English army lost a big fight on the Hudson River. Parliament heard about this fight. So it sent men to the Continental Congress. These men said that the colonists would not have to obey some laws of Parliament. They also said that the Patriots would not have to go to jail. But the colonists would have to stop their fights against the English army.

General Washington fought against the English army.

By 1777, the colonists and the English army had been fighting for a long time. Many colonists did not want to obey any laws of Parliament. They wanted to make their own laws. These colonists wanted their independence. So they would not stop the Revolution.

France wanted to fight against England. France thought that the war in the colonies would hurt England. In 1778, France and the Continental Congress said that they would help each other. They wrote a treaty. In this treaty, France said that the colonies should have their independence from England. It also said that France would help the colonies. The colonists would try to keep the French West Indies safe. For two years, France helped the colonists in their Revolution. France sent guns, men, and money to the colonies.

The Revolution took eight years. The colonists had many troubles. Many colonists did not want to fight for so long in this war. Some merchants and farmers sold their things at high prices. They did not help the soldiers. The colonists and the army had to pay a lot of money for things. Other merchants and farmers helped the army. Some of them even gave money to the army. Then the army could have more food and clothes. They could fight better against the English army.

Some people in England thought that the colonies could have their independence. They did not think that England had to have so many colonies. Many men in England did not want to be soldiers in the English army. They did not want to fight against the colonists. But England needed a large army. So the king of England paid men from other countries. They became soldiers in the English army. These soldiers did not care about the Revolution. They did not fight well.

Not all the colonists wanted the Revolution. Some of them even helped the English army. Some of them asked the first Americans to help the English army. Some first Americans did not want the colonists to take all their land. Parliament had told them that the colonists could not live west of the Appalachian Mountains. The first Americans wanted the colonies to stay small. So some first Americans also fought against the colonists.

The End of the Revolution

In the summer of 1781, Washington and the American army met the English army in Yorktown, Virginia. They fought. The French navy helped the American army. The French ships were in the ocean near Yorktown. They would not let the English army leave Yorktown. At last, the colonists won the Revolution. The general of the English army said that his soldiers would not fight in the Revolution anymore. The Revolution was over. The colonists won their independence. The colonies would not be part of England anymore.

A few days later, all the men in the Second Continental Congress knew that the colonists had won the Revolution. The congress sent a few men to Paris, France. These men talked to representatives from the governments of England, France, and Spain. All these men talked about a treaty. Then England and the colonies would know what they had to do. It took two years to write this treaty.

In 1783, men from England and the colonies wrote a treaty. It said that the colonies could have their independence. It also said that the colonists could live in the land between the Appalachian Mountains and the Mississippi River. England still owned the land north of the St. Lawrence River. Today, this land is called Canada.